John Thompson's Easiest Piano Course

PART THREE

Exclusive distributors:
Music Sales Limited, 8-9 Frith Street, London W1V 5TZ.
Music Sales Pty Limited, 120 Rothschild Avenue, Rosebery, NSW 2018, Australia.

Order No. WMR000319

Printed and bound in the United Kingdom by Printwise (Haverhill) Limited, Haverhill, Suffolk.

This publication is not for sale in the United States of America and/or Canada

The Willis Music Co.

Contents

Foreword

THE PHRASE

PART THREE begins by showing the importance of thinking and feeling music phrase by phrase rather than note by note.

Teachers should emphasize the matter of playing each phrase with different musical treatment—one of the first steps in Interpretation.

TOUCH

TOUCH is obviously a vital part of Interpretation and examples in *staccato*, *legato*, slurs, etc., follow in proper sequence.

For thorough development of the various Touches, the teacher is referred to the author's edition of the HANON STUDIES—now adopted as a standard part of the teaching equipment of most piano teachers and music schools.

SCALES AND CHORDS

Scale formation follows the lessons on Semitones and Whole Tones, with examples using the scale both as Melody and as accompaniment figures.

Later Triads and Inversions are shown with pieces employing chord figures in 'block' and broken form.

The 7th chord (with its resolution) is not analysed harmonically, but simply taught as a CHORD PATTERN which should be memorized by the pupil because of its frequent appearance in music of this grade.

BOOGIE WOOGIE

Many teachers may be startled because of the inclusion of Boogie Woogie and other numbers having a popular 'flavour'.

But it must be admitted that Popular Music is here to stay—and why not? It has a very definite place of its own in the world of music. And whether we approve or not, our pupils will be exposed to it daily on radio, television, gramophone, cafés, etc.

Perhaps for that very reason it may even be a *duty* of the so-called "long-haired" musician to teach Young players how to distinguish between good and bad Popular Music!

In any event, the majority of piano pupils take up music, not as a career, but as a *means of entertainment* —which by the way, is the prime purpose of *all* music, classic or otherwise. The author, therefore, feels no need to apologize for the popular type of some of the examples. If they do nothing else, they at least show that Boogie Woogie, Rag Time, etc., are not new inventions in the popular field, but are simply exaggerated use of devices known to the classic composers many years ago.

It should be noted, however, that even the "pop" examples have a definite purpose and develop either a technical or musical point of pianism.

SCOPE

In Key Signatures, the book progresses as far as three flats and three sharps. The remaining Key Signatures follow in proper order in PART FOUR.

On page 44 the scales and chords used in the book are shown for reference.

A Glossary of musical terms, with abbreviations and definitions will be found on page 45.

The last few lessons in the book present SIX-EIGHT—a new Time Signature so far.

As with the other books in this Course, the lessons are specially designed for the short practice periods of present-day pupils.

John Thompson

Hand Position

Preparatory Studies

Melody

1st Phrase

2nd Phrase

The Phrase

Music, like language, is divided into sentences, but musical sentences are called PHRASES.

The above example consists of two phrases. Sometimes the second phrase is played louder than the first —sometimes softer. But never exactly alike.

How do *you* think the second phrase should be played? It is correct either way, but it should be played the way *you* feel it. Always think of your Music *phrase by phrase*, not note by note. Then you will play with more musical purpose and understanding.

Three Phrases

Hand Position

Here is a piece with three phrases. Try playing it three different ways.

First time—1st phrase, very softly; 2nd phrase, somewhat louder; 3rd phrase, still louder.

Second time—1st phrase, moderately loud; 2nd phrase, softly; 3rd phrase, much louder.

Third time—1st phrase, moderately loud; 2nd phrase, somewhat softer; 3rd phrase, much softer.

Choose the way you like best. That will be *your very own* interpretation.

Preparatory Studies

The Bee

1st Phrase

Folk Song

2nd Phrase

3rd Phrase

Four Phrases

This piece has four phrases.

Notice that each phrase is marked differently.

Usually the composer indicates how each phrase should be played. When no expression marks are shown, play according to *your* feeling.

An explanation of all musical terms used in this book will be found on page 45.

BE SURE TO LOOK THEM UP.

Much Ado About Nothing

Wrist Staccato

TEACHERS' NOTE—The subject of *Touch* is too vital to be treated as part of a Grade Book.

It is suggested that the pupil be assigned at this poinr, the author's HANON STUDIES which are specially adapted for students in this grade. Each Touch is carefully explained and developed separately.

Obviously, TOUCH is an important part of Interpretation and should be introduced early in the pupil's career.

Finger, Wrist and *Forearm staccato* as well as the various forms of *Finger legato, phrasing* and *portamento* playing, all in elementary form, are treated in the JOHN THOMPSON HANON STUDIES.

For playing the following examples give the pupil your favourite demonstration of Wrist Staccato.

Exercise in Wrist Staccato

Allegro

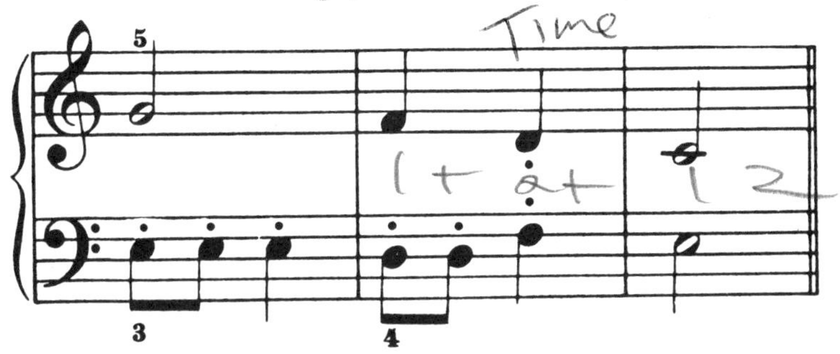

ALWAYS BE SURE TO NOTICE THE EXPRESSION MARKS. SEE PAGE 45.

Some Folks Do

Adapted from Stephen Foster

Allegretto

Homework
14/11/96

Work Sheet

Exercise in naming and transposing the new notes 

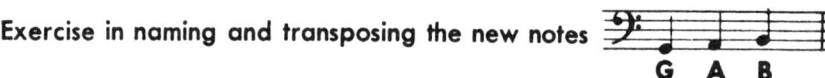

Write the letter names below.

Writing Exercise

Transpose these notes one octave higher in the Bass.

Next write them in the Treble Clef.

Then recite them as you play.

At the Animal Fair

You must count time, don't ignore the 3 rests

(Study in Wrist Staccato)

there. The old ra - coon by the light of the moon was
comb-ing his au - burn hair. The mon - key went ker -
plunk, Fell o - ver the el - e-phant's trunk. The el - e-phant
sneezed, Fell down on his knees, So what be - came of the monk!
G

CHANGING HAND POSITION

Up to this point you have changed Hand Position frequently when moving from one piece to another.

You will find it is just as easy to change position *in the middle* of a piece, and that is what happens in "On the Levee." See how smoothly you can make the change.

On the Levee

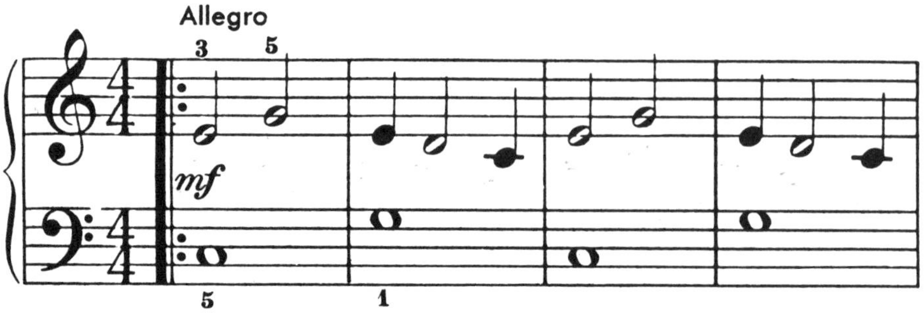

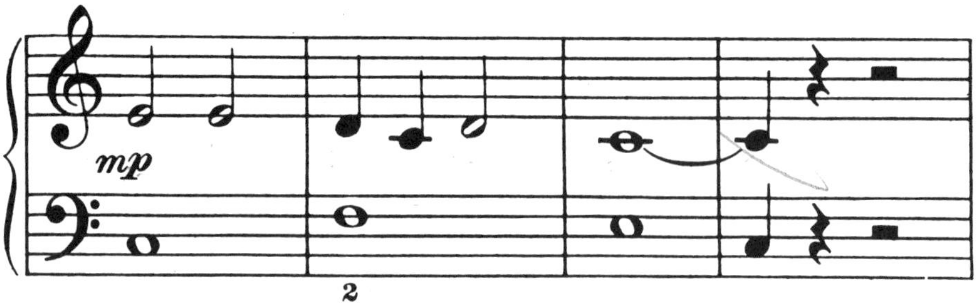

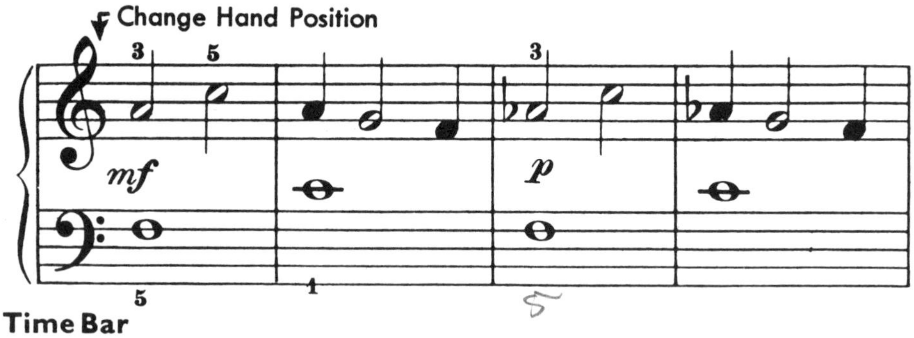

FIRST AND SECOND TIME BARS

From this point, go back to the beginning and play over again.

After playing through the SECOND time, do NOT repeat the FIRST TIME BAR; instead, skip to the SECOND TIME BAR.

Sunrise

NEW EXPRESSION MARKS

means a gradual increase in tone.

means a gradual decrease in tone.

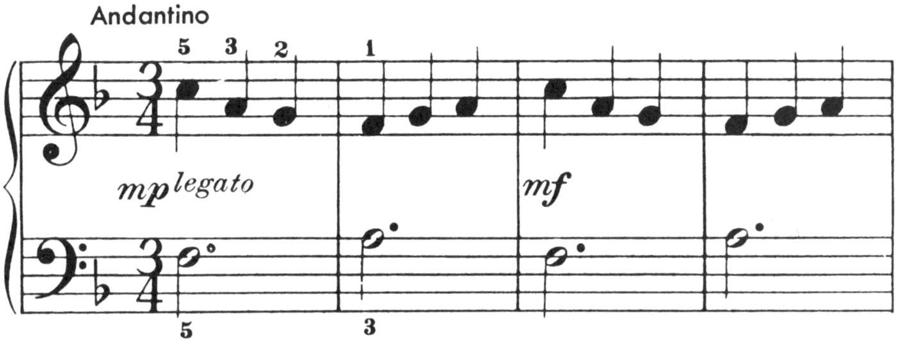

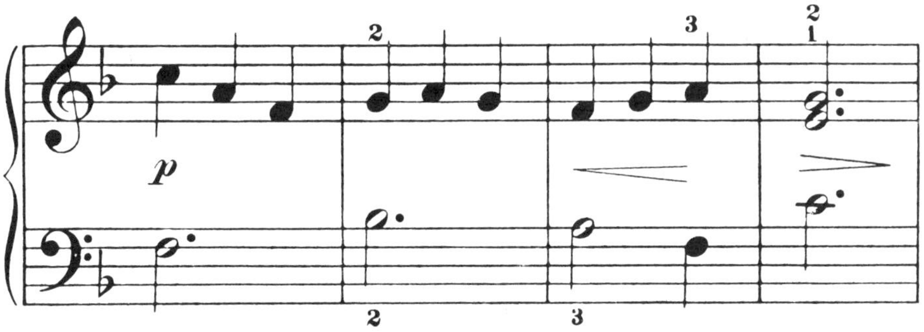

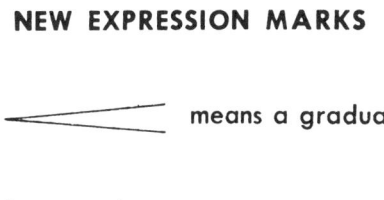

The Slur

SLURRING in music is like BREATHING in speech—we take *short breaths* and *long breaths.* If we keep in mind to make our playing of music BREATHE AT THE END OF EACH SLUR, it will strengthen the rhythm and add immensely to the interpretation.

In playing TWO-NOTE SLURS think of the words, DROP-ROLL and the effect will come naturally. In the following example, play the *first* note with a gentle DROP of the arm and the *second* note with a ROLL of the arm and hand in an inward and upward motion, *using no finger action* and *releasing the note* on the upward roll.

The following illustration shows the proper position of hand and arm as each Slur is released. The WRIST must be completely relaxed.

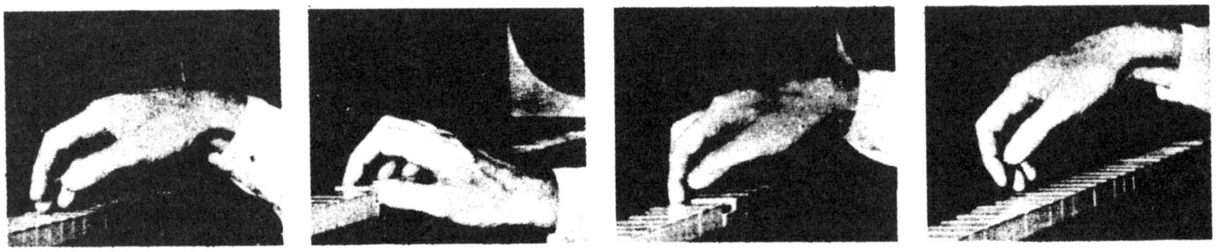

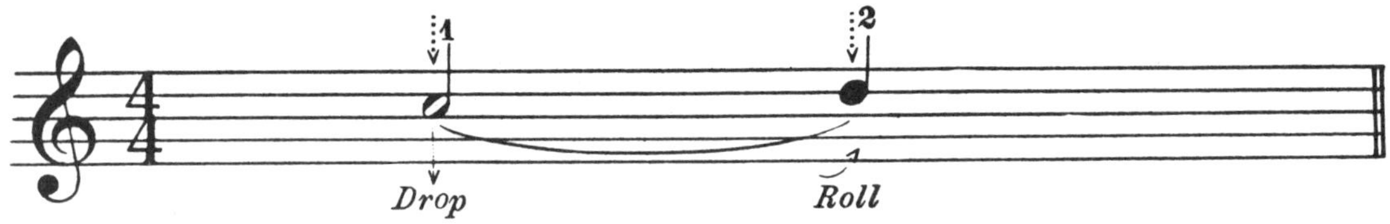

Play the following with the RIGHT hand

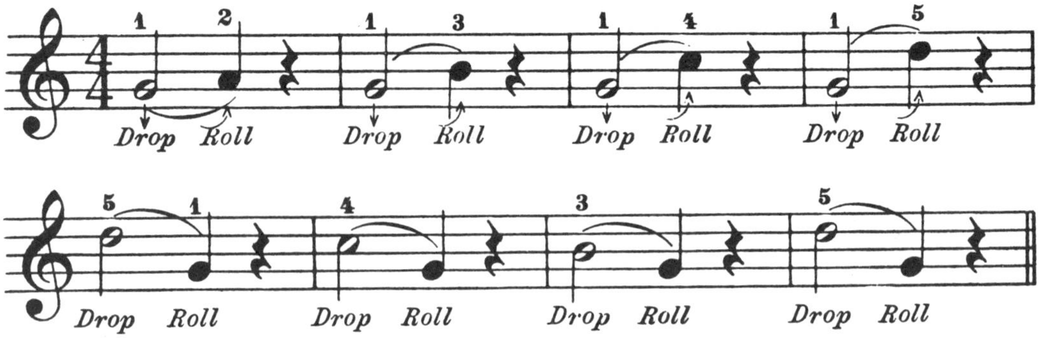

Play the following with the LEFT hand

The SIGN of the Slur is the curved line, . All notes under this line, except the last one, should be played LEGATO. The last note must always be played with a rolling motion of the arm *forward* and *upward.*

> *"The HANON Studies" by John Thompson should be assigned as supplementary work. This book is issued with attractive titles and illustrations, and is especially adapted for this grade to develop the SLURRING ATTACK as well as all the fundamental touches used in this book.*

Pop Goes the Weasel

Be Sure

To observe the many two-note slurs (*drop-roll*).

Also the *accent* and *staccato notes* on the last line.

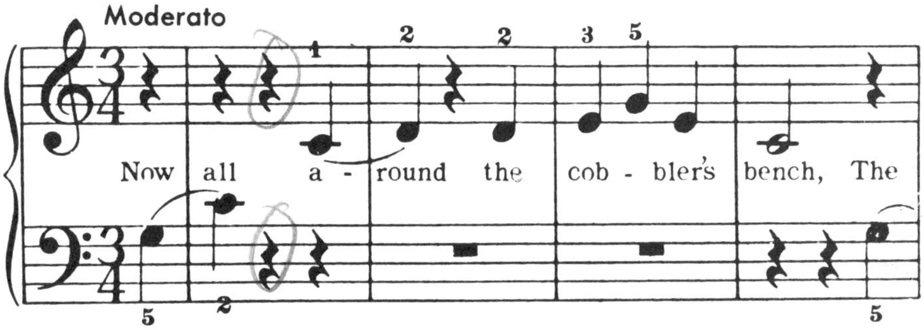
Moderato
Now all a - round the cob - bler's bench, The

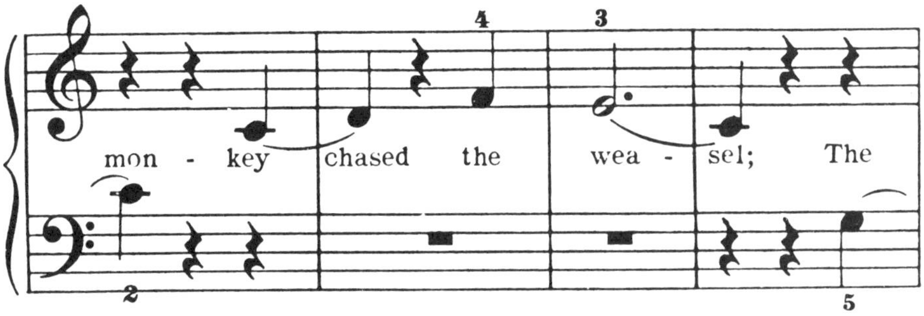
mon - key chased the wea - sel; The

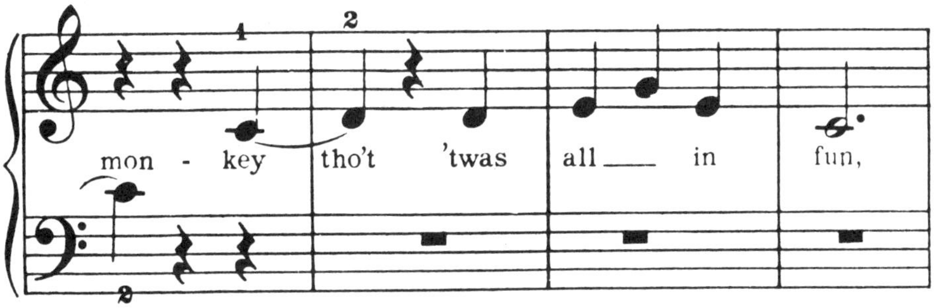
mon - key tho't 'twas all in fun,

f
Pop!
left hand over
goes the wea - sel.

Accompaniment

1.
2.

Preparatory Exercise

Boogie Woogie Bill

Allegro Moderato

Robin Redbreast

SEMITONES (Half Steps)

A SEMITONE is the distance between any key and its *next nearest key.*

Play the following progression, using the second finger of the right hand, thus,

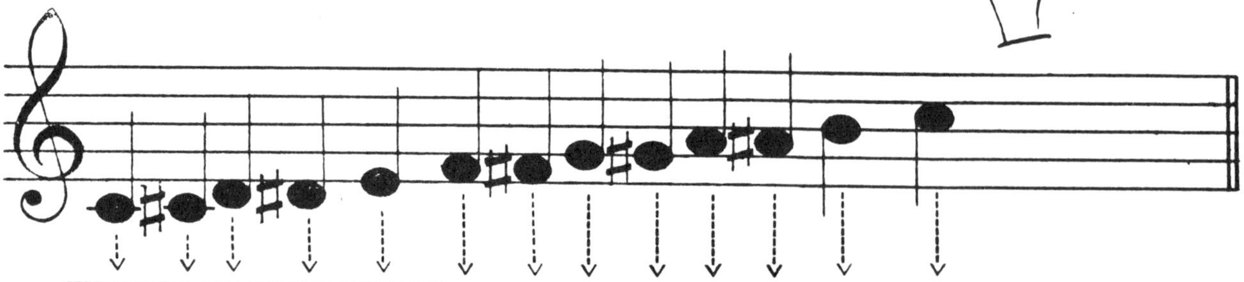

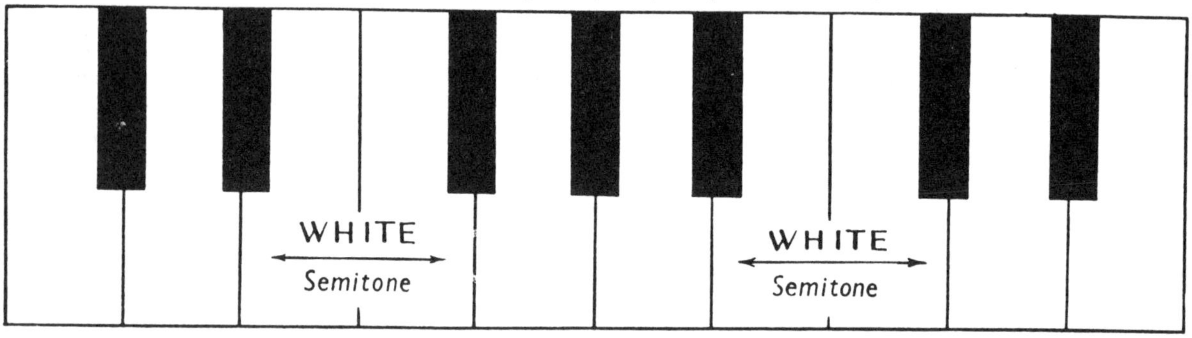

You have played a series of Semitones.

Notice that the piano keyboard is arranged in Semitones.

All semitones occur between a White Key and a Black Key, EXCEPT the two WHITE SEMITONES between E and F and B and C.

Play these descending semitones with the left hand second finger.

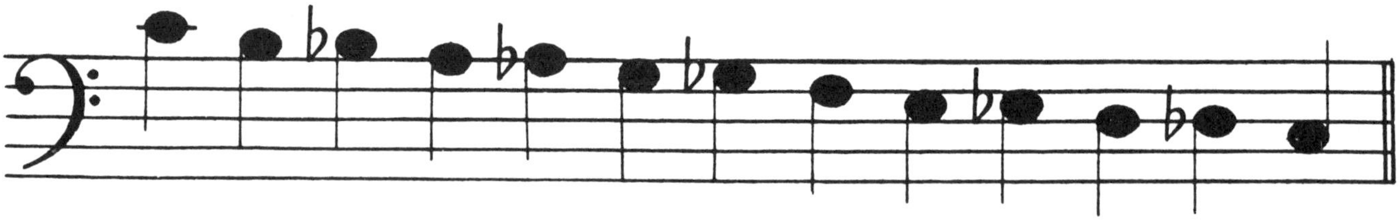

Review

You have already learned that:

A SHARP (♯) placed before a note, *raises* it a semitone.

A FLAT (♭) placed before a note, *lowers* it a semitone.

A NATURAL (♮) placed before a note, *cancels* the sharp or flat sign.

WHOLE TONES (Whole Steps)

A WHOLE TONE is twice the distance of a semitone.

Therefore there will always be one key—either Black or White—lying in between.

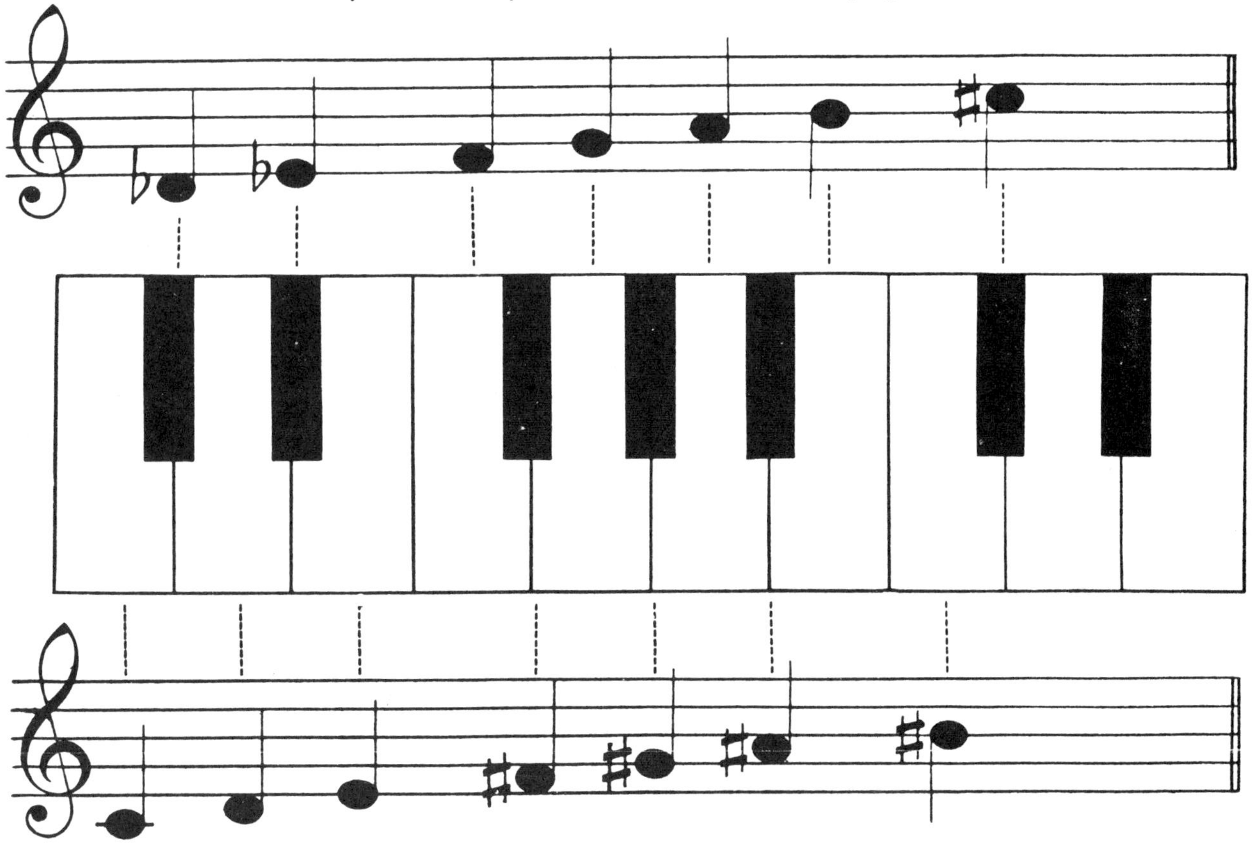

WHOLE TONES AND SEMITONES

Define the following examples as whole tones or semitones.

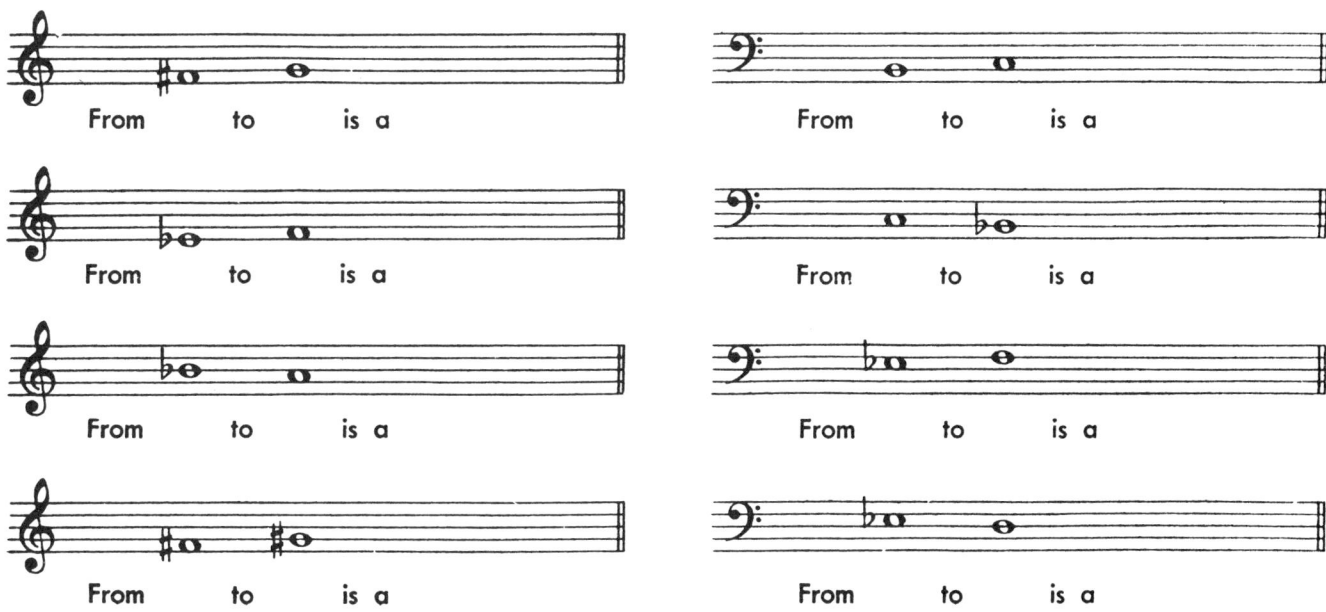

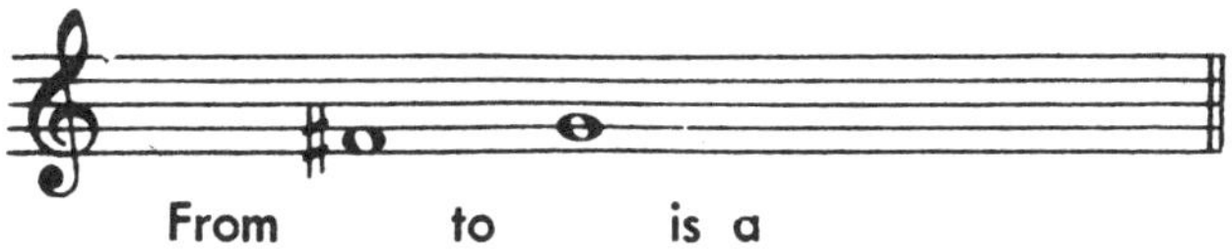

From to is a

From to is a

From to is a

From to is a

From to is a

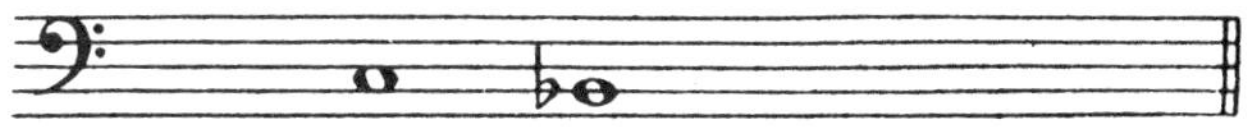

From to is a

From to is a

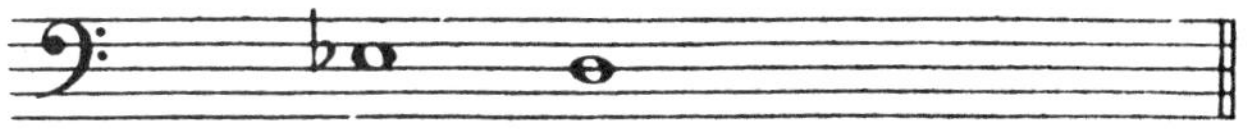

From to is a

Three-note Slur

Drop—Connect—Roll

To play a three-note slur, DROP on the first note, CONNECT the second with finger legato and ROLL off on the third note.

Shufflin' Along

(Boogie Woogie)

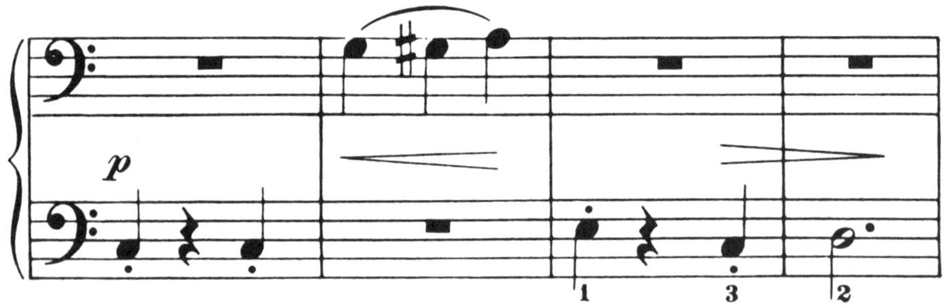

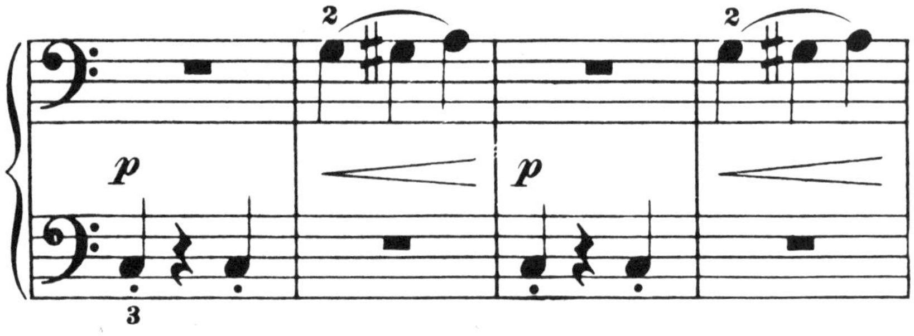

BOOGIE WOOGIE

BOOGIE WOOGIE is a term used in Popular Music for *repeated patterns* —a device known and used in Standard Music almost since its origin.

About the only difference is that Popular Music repeats the figures more often than would be considered good taste in what we look upon as Standard Music.

This is the second "Boogie Woogie" tune you have had in this book.

The first was "BOOGIE WOOGIE BILL" in which the repeated pattern was used as accompaniment. Here it appears as melody and is repeated over and over with monotonous regularity.

Cross-Hand Piece

Here is a cross-hand piece, built for the most part, on three-note slurs.

Make as much distinction as possible between *staccato* and *legato*.

Be careful of the expression marks and see if you can imitate the playfulness of **dancing shadows.**

Shadow Dance

Major Scales

Writing Exercises

A scale is a succession of eight notes progressing in alphabetical order.

The notes are numbered **1, 2, 3, 4, 5, 6, 7, 8** and are known as the degrees of the scale.

The Major Scale contains whole tones and semitones.

The semitones occur between **3** and **4** and between **7** and **8** as shown in the example which follows.

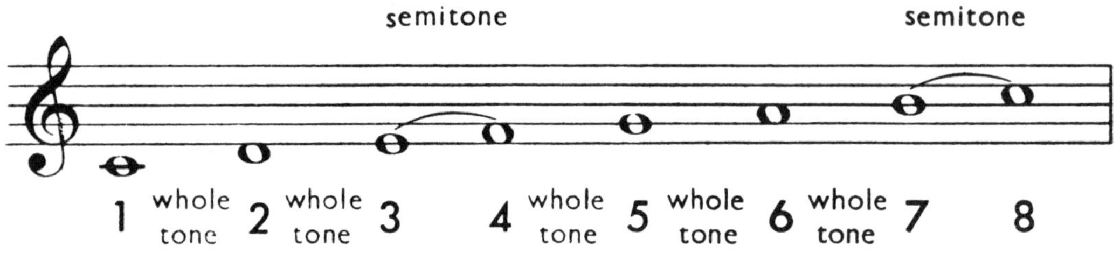

Write the following scales using sharps or flats as needed to preserve the order of whole tones and semitones.

Scale of G Major

Scale of F Major

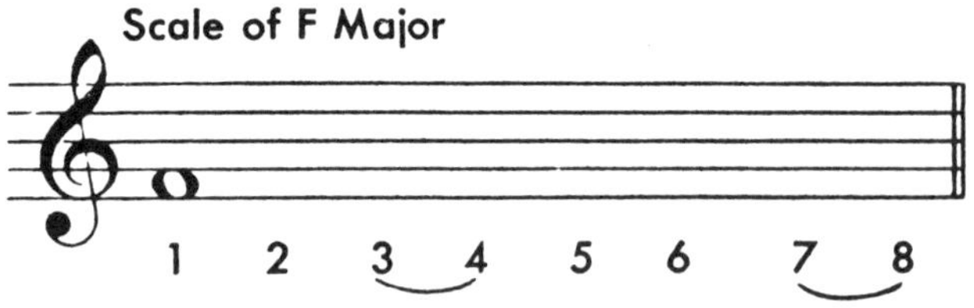

Scale of D Major

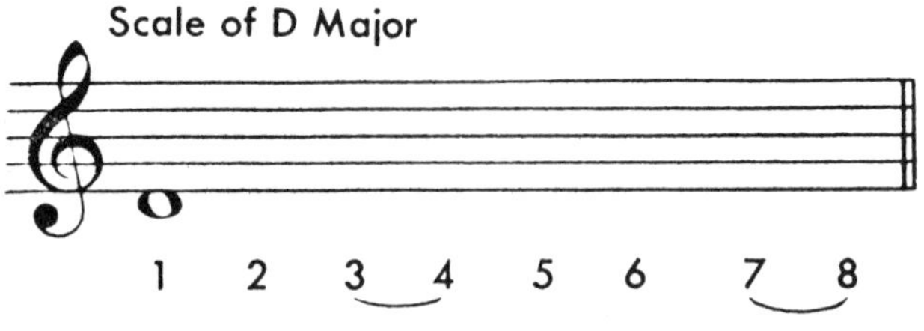

Scale of B♭ Major

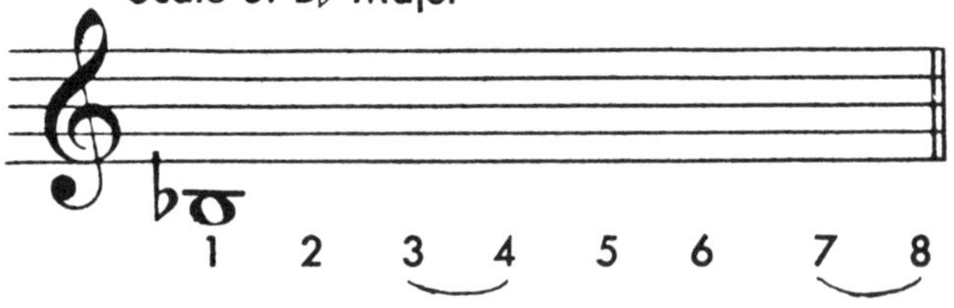

Scale of A Major

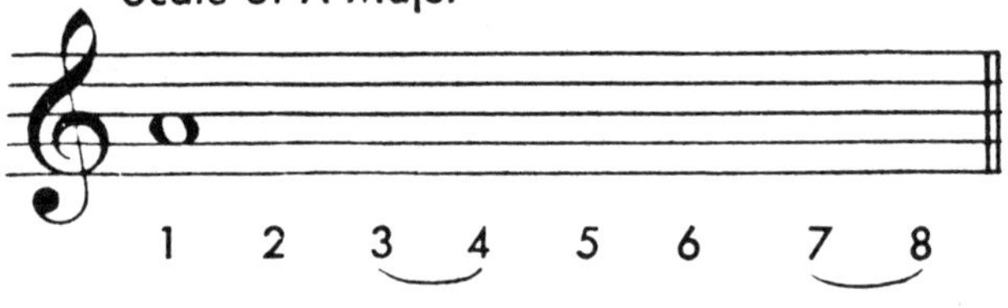

Scale of E♭ Major

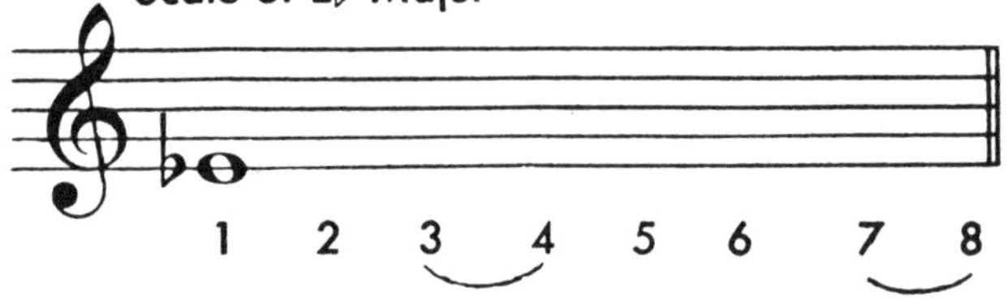

Preparatory Exercise

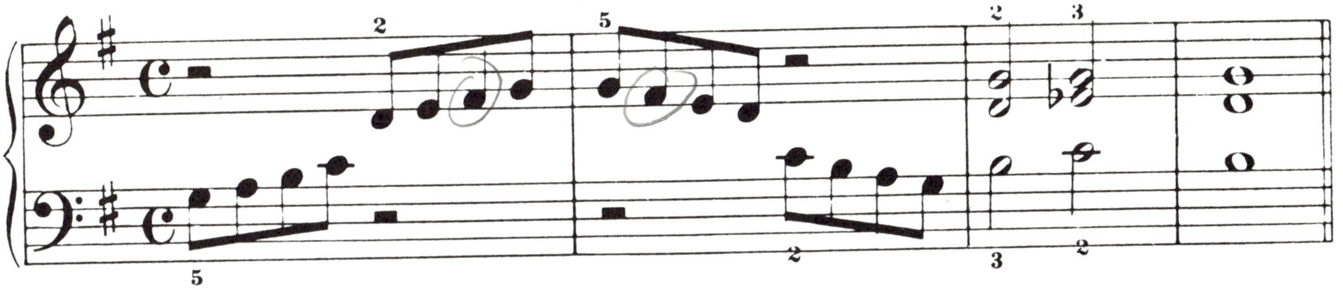

New Signature for Four-Four

The sign **C**, is just another way of showing the Time Signature of Four-Four.

In the following example, you will find the G major scale, divided between the hands, and used as Melody.

Steady, even, Pulse.

The Juggler

5/2/97

Scale Drill

Allegro

Acrobats

Allegro animato

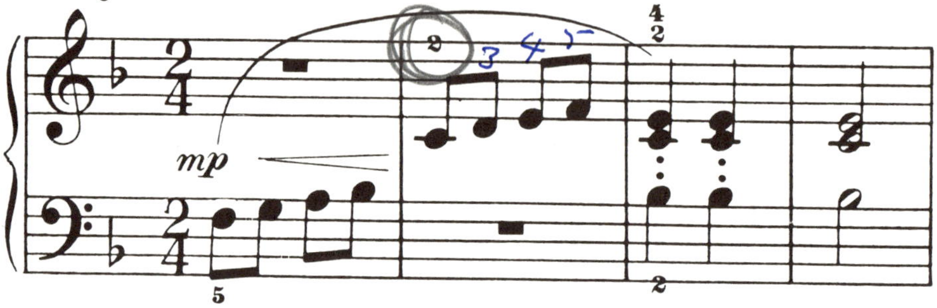

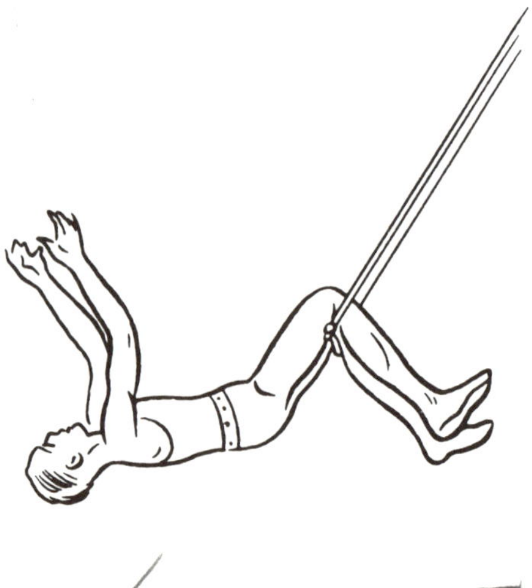

Syncopation

I Like Rhythm

I like Rhythm in all my livin',
A tune with Rhythm is just for me.
Syncopation has got the Nation,
But it's as easy as "A B C."

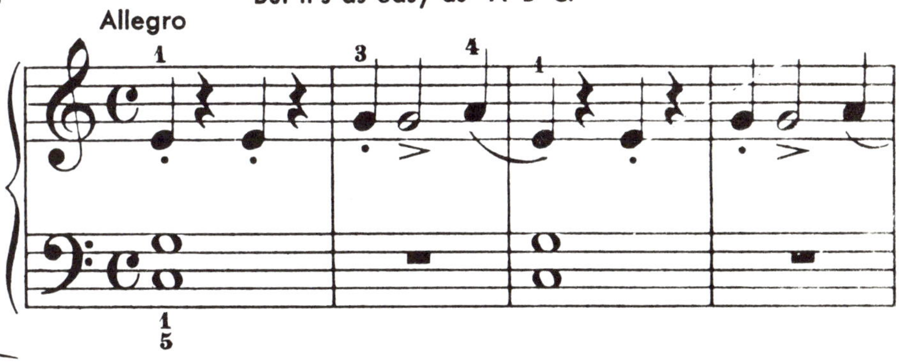

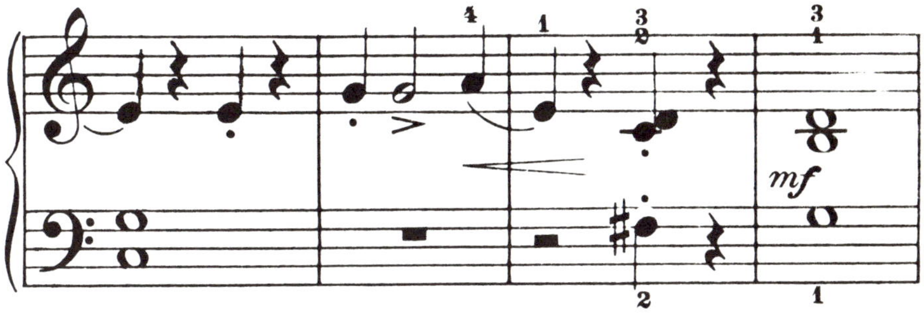

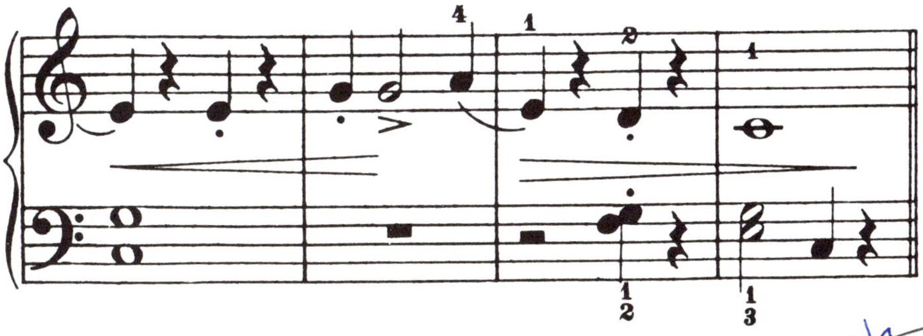

SYNCOPATION

SYNCOPATION is a term usually thought of as belonging only to Popular Music. However, it was used in the Classics hundreds of years ago.

The only thing new about it is its over-use. In Classical or Standard Music it is used sparingly—in Popular Music it is employed in almost every bar.

Syncopation occurs when the normal accent has been disturbed. That is, when the accent is placed on a beat that would ordinarily be a weak beat.

In this example we find the second beat (normally a weak beat) emphasized by the accent sign. This change of accent gives a "swing" to the rhythm known as Syncopation.

Preparatory Exercise

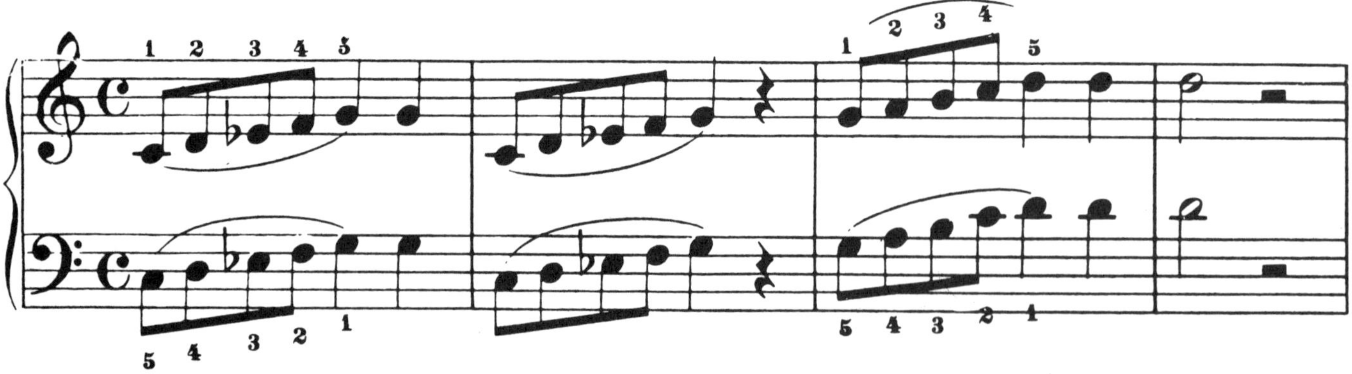

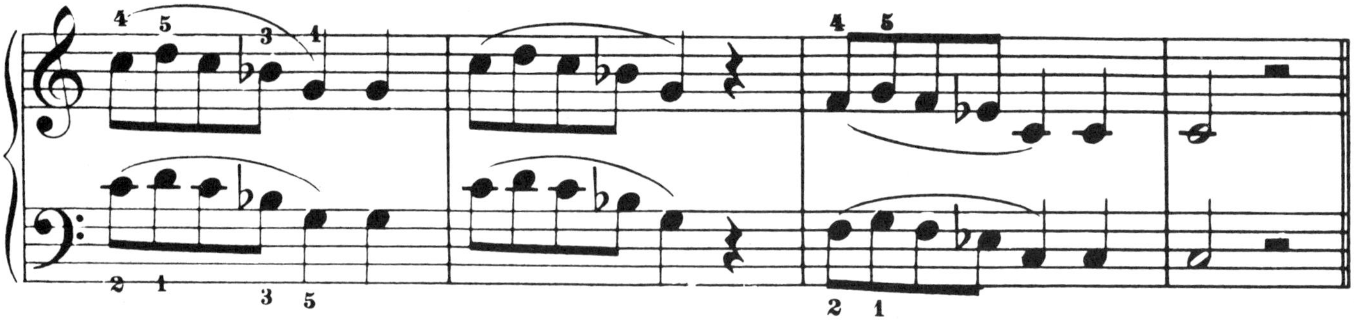

Tribal Dance

Allegro

f
mf
mp
p
pp
8

Duet for Teacher and Pupil

Cake Walk

Secondo

The CAKE WALK is an institution of by-gone days. It was performed by couples marching around the dance floor to the music of the band.

At intervals along the march, a flag was passed from one couple to the next, and when the band stopped playing—without warning—the couple then holding the flag was entitled to win the prize, which was, of course, a cake. It was particularly popular in the South among the Negroes. The music was "rag-time" in character and well adapted to the complicated steps and body gyrations, in which each couple tried to out-do the others.

In this example the syncopation occurs on the last half of the first beat in most of the bars. Be sure to apply vigorous accents throughout.

Cake Walk

Jenny you Must Count time.

Chord - Building

Major Triads

A TRIAD is a chord of *three notes.*

If you take the 1st, 3rd and 5th notes of the Major Scale (skipping those in between)

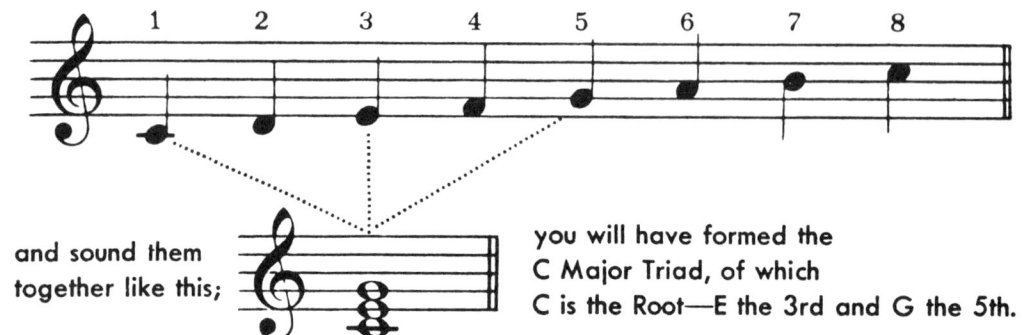

and sound them together like this;

you will have formed the C Major Triad, of which C is the Root—E the 3rd and G the 5th.

Play these Triads

the F Major Triad

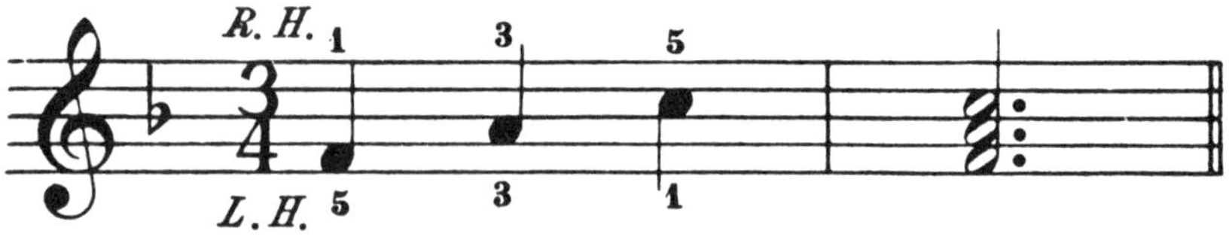

the G Major Triad

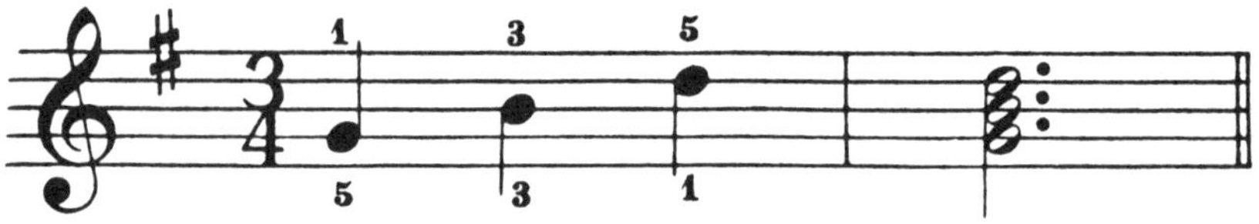

Broken Triads

When Triads appear in broken form, they are known as Broken Chords or *Arpeggios.*

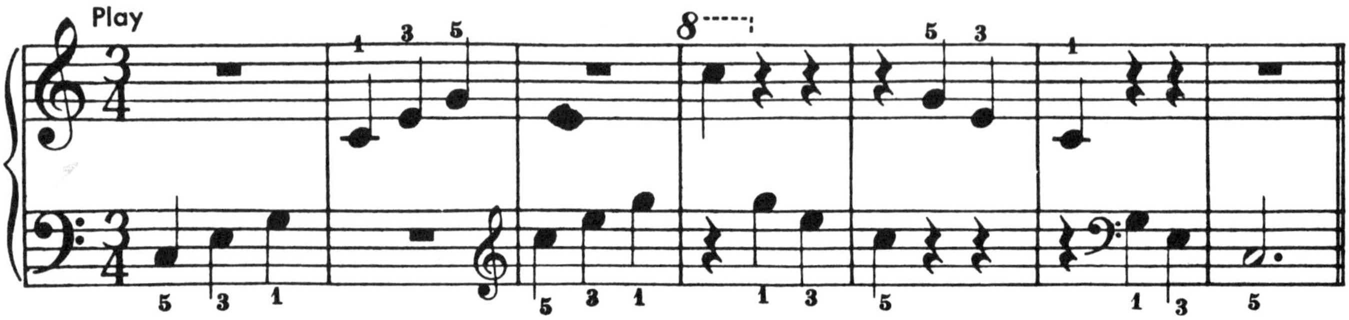

Play the F Major and G Major Arpeggios in the form shown above.

Inversions

Sometimes the notes of a Triad are "scrambled" like the words in a puzzle—in which case they are said to be INVERTED.

The Three Positions of the C Major Triad

(Play)

Root Position

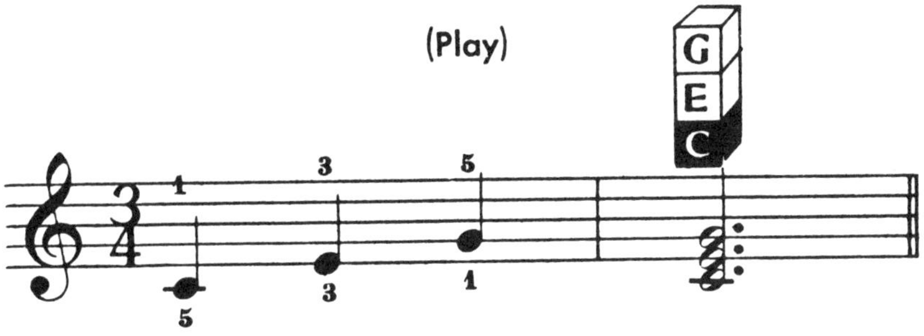

Root on the bottom

First Inversion

Root on top

Second Inversion

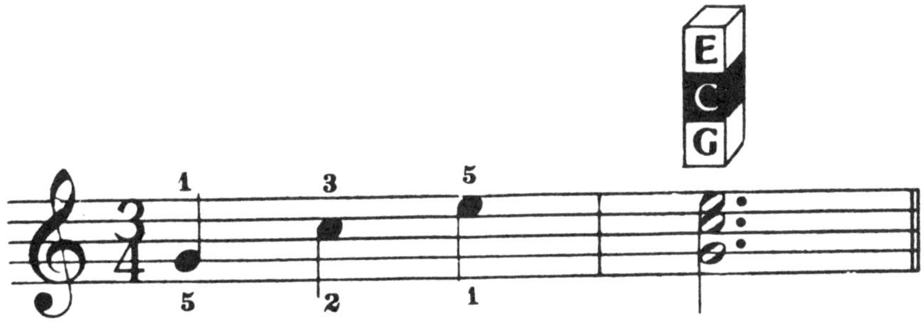

Root in the middle

Write (and play) the three positions of the F Major and G Major Triads—using the same chord patterns as shown in the examples above.

Root Position | First Inversion | Second Inversion

F Major

G Major

Chord Capers

17/4/97

Broken Chord Etude

Chord Patterns

Here are some Chord Patterns that will appear frequently in your music.

Play them over many times until you can recognize them by sight and by ear.

This will help your Sight Reading and Memorizing.

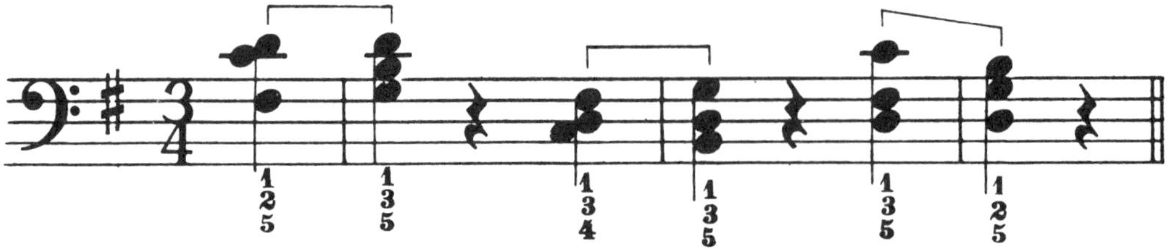

An Old Folk Tune

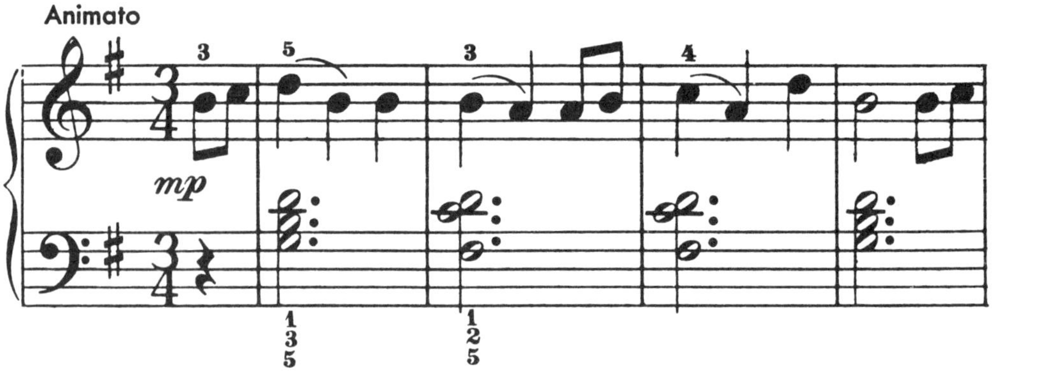

Cross-Hand Etude

On Broken Chords

Allegretto

Dissonances

The music of the Orient is apt to sound discordant to our ears.

That is because of the many dissonances used.

However, there is a certain beauty to dissonances which you will learn to appreciate as you advance in your piano study.

Meantime, here is an imitation of Oriental music.

Chinese Theatre

Play the scale and arpeggio of D Major each day before practising this piece.

Scales in all keys used in this book are shown on page 44.

Be sure to observe the many two-note slurs in this piece.

Apply sharp accents on the first of each bar to ensure good rhythm.

Peasant Dance

Animato

Folk Tune

W.M.Co. 7261

Play this etude in two ways. First time, as written—2 notes with the left hand and 3 with the right. Second time, make a cross-hand study of it by passing the left hand over to play the last note of each bar with the second finger. (This applies to all bars except the last two)

In bars 10, 11, 12 and 13, play the notes with the little lines under them (𝅗𝅥) with extra singing quality—almost like melody notes.

Pedal may be used— once to each bar —at the discretion of the teacher.

Etude in B Flat

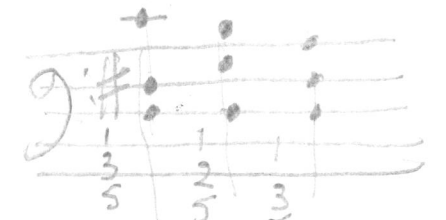

Play this old Italian song as expressively as possible.

The left hand broken chords should be played with a rolling motion of the hand from the fifth finger over to the thumb.

Keep moving along gently.

In a Gondola

Cowboy's Song

Andantino
Last night as I rode o'er the prai-rie, And looked at the stars in the sky. I won-dered if ev-er a cow-boy Would drift to that sweet by-and-by.
Roll on, Roll on, Roll on lit-tle do-gies, roll on, roll on. on.

A Little Bit of Rag

Preparatory Study

A major scale

Holiday Song

Animato

Play the A major Scale and Arpeggio daily.

Six-Eight

Here is a new Time Signature which means there are *six counts to each* bar and one count to each quaver.

Time Values are as follows

♪ = 1 count	
♩ = 2 counts	𝅗𝅥 = 4 counts
♩. = 3 counts	𝅗𝅥. = 6 counts

There are two accents to the bar ——a strong one on the first count and a weaker one on the fourth count.

Tramp, Tramp, Tramp

Vivace

George F. Root

f
Tramp! tramp! tramp! the boys are march ing,
Cheer up com - rades they will come,
And be - neath the star - ry flag, We shall breathe the air a - gain, Of the
free land in our own be - lov - ed home.

Hand Position

By Moonlight

How D'ye Do?

Allegro animato

SCALES and CHORDS

Used in this Book

C Major

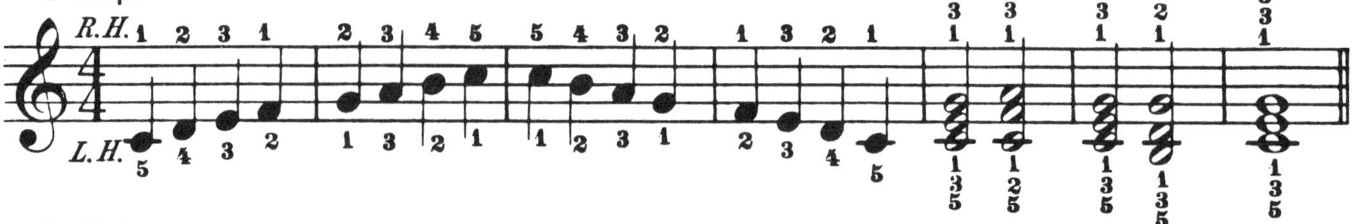

G Major

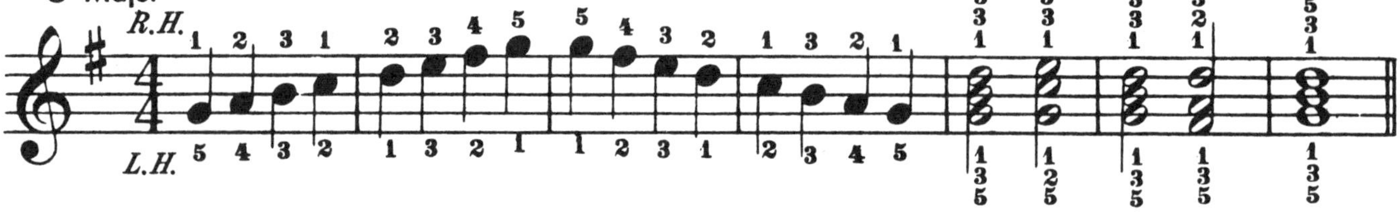

D Major

A Major

F Major

B♭ Major

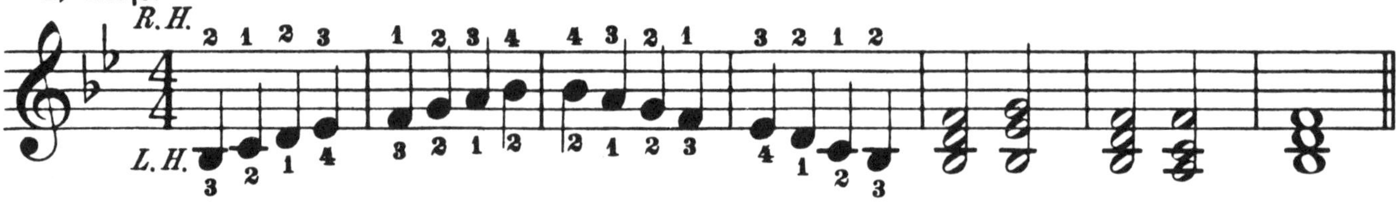

E♭ Major

GLOSSARY

of

Musical Terms and Expression Marks

Used in this book.

> — **Accent** . . . Special emphasis on a note or chord

Allegretto . . . Light and Lively

Allegro . . . Fast

Andante . . . Slow

Andantino . . . Slow, but not as slow as Andante

Animato . . . Animated

a tempo . . . Return to original speed

 — **Crescendo** . . . Gradually louder

 — **Decrescendo** . . . Gradually softer

Diminuendo . . . Softer by degrees

f — **Forte** . . . Loud

ff — **Fortissimo** . . . Very loud

Legato . . . Smooth and connected

L.H. . . . Left Hand

8va . . . Play one octave higher

mf — **Mezzo Forte** . . . Moderately loud

mp — **Mezzo Piano** . . . Moderately soft

Moderato . . . Moderately fast

 — **Pause** . . . Hold the note or chord longer according to taste

pp — **Pianissimo** . . . Very soft

p — **Piano** . . . Soft

Poco . . . Little

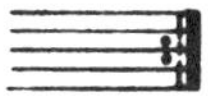 Repeat Sign

R.H. . . . Right Hand

Rit . . . **Ritard** . . . Slower by degrees

 — **Slur** . . . Connected

Staccato . . . Detached, short

Tempo . . . Rate of speed

Vivace . . . Fast and vivacious

Printed in Great Britain by Commercial Colour Press, 3/96 (23919)

Certificate of Merit

This certifies that

....

has successfully completed

PART THREE

OF

John Thompson's
EASIEST PIANO COURSE

and is eligible for promotion to

PART FOUR

....

Teacher

Date..